CONTENTS

AFRICA BY COUNTRY

Although many people speak of Africa as if it were a single country, Africa is just like Europe in that it is made up of a great many separate states with their own traditions and identities.

NORTH AND WEST AFRICA

The countries of North Africa face the Mediterranean Sea. In centuries gone by, travel by sea was often easier than by land and so many of these countries have had close links with countries across the Mediterranean. Despite the challenges posed by the enormous Sahara Desert to the south, the Berbers and Arabs who lived in North Africa developed trade routes with settlements right across the other side.

MOROCCO
Capital: Rabat
Area: 446,550 km²
Population: 27,377,000
Currency: Dirham
GNP per person (US$): 1260
Principal languages: Arabic

WESTERN SAHARA
Capital: el-Aaiun
Area: 266,000 km²
Population: 275,000
Currency: Dirham
GNP per person (US$): 1030
Principal languages: Arabic

MAURITANIA
Capital: Nouakchott
Area: 1,025,520 km²
Population: 2,529,000
Currency: Ouguiya
GNP per person (US$): 440
Principal languages: Arabic/French

CAPE VERDE
Capital: Praia
Area: 4,033 km²
Population: 408,000
Currency: Escudo
GNP per person (US$): 1090
Principal languages: Portuguese

SENEGAL
Capital: Dakar
Area: 196,192 km²
Population: 9,003,000
Currency: CFA franc
GNP per person (US$): 540
Principal languages: Wolof/French

THE GAMBIA
Capital: Banjul
Area: 10,689 km²
Population: 1,229,000
Currency: Dalasi
GNP per person (US$): 340
Principal languages: English

MALI
Capital: Bamako
Area: 1,248,574 km²
Population: 10,694,000
Currency: CFA franc
GNP per person (US$): 260
Principal languages: Bambara/French

GUINEA-BISSAU
Capital: Bissau
Area: 36,125 km²
Population: 1,161,000
Currency: Peso
GNP per person (US$): 230
Principal languages: Portuguese

IVORY COAST
Capital: Abidjan
Area: 322,500 km²
Population: 14,292,000
Currency: CFA franc
GNP per person (US$): 710
Principal languages: French

BURKINA FASO
Capital: Ouagadougou
Area: 274,220 km²
Population: 11,305,000
Currency: CFA franc
GNP per person (US$): 250
Principal languages: French/Mossi

GUINEA
Capital: Conakry
Area: 245,857 km²
Population: 7,337,000
Currency: Franc
GNP per person (US$): 550
Principal languages: French

LIBERIA
Capital: Monrovia
Area: 112,600 km²
Population: 2,666,000
Currency: Dollar
GNP per person (US$): 490
Principal languages: Kpelle/English

GHANA
Capital: Accra
Area: 238,533 km²
Population: 19,162,000
Currency: Cedi
GNP per person (US$): 390
Principal languages: English/Twi/Fanti

SIERRA LEONE
Capital: Freetown
Area: 72,325 km²
Population: 4,568,000
Currency: Leone
GNP per person (US$): 160
Principal languages: Mende/English

CONTINENTS

AFRICA

Regan & Cremin

HODDER
Wayland

an imprint of Hodder Children's Books

CONTINENTS series includes:

AFRICA
AUSTRALIA & OCEANIA

EUROPE
NORTH AMERICA

First published in Great Britain in 1996 by Wayland Publishers
Ltd. This updated paperback edition published in 2000 by
Hodder Wayland, an imprint of Hodder Children's Books.

A Catalogue record for this book is available from the British
Library.

ISBN 0 7502 2835 0

Printed and bound in Italy by G. Canale & C. S.p.A.

Hodder Children's Books
A division of Hodder Headline plc
338 Euston Road, London NW1 3BH

Statistics
Population figures, life expectancy and infant mortality figures
in this book are for 1998.
Literacy rates are for 1995.
GNP figures are for 1997.

Sources
United Nations Development Programme
Unicef: *The State of the World's Children, 2000*

Picture credits: Britstock 13; Camera Press 42; Hutchinson
15, 19, 36, 37, 37, 39; Impact 26, 43; Panos 22, 25, 31, 32, 33;
Spectrum Colour Library 17; Trip 12, 14, 17, 23, 27, 38–39, 41;
Frank Spooner Pictures 11, 23, 27, 29; Wayland Picture Library
19, 20, 24, 26, 28, 29, 34, 35, 40; Zefa, contents page, 10

Maps by Peter Bull. Graph artwork by Mark Whitchurch.

The countries of West Africa range from the desert lands of Mauritania and Western Sahara, which have relatively small populations, to the much more populous equatorial lands bordering the Gulf of Guinea. This area includes Africa's most densely populated country, Nigeria.

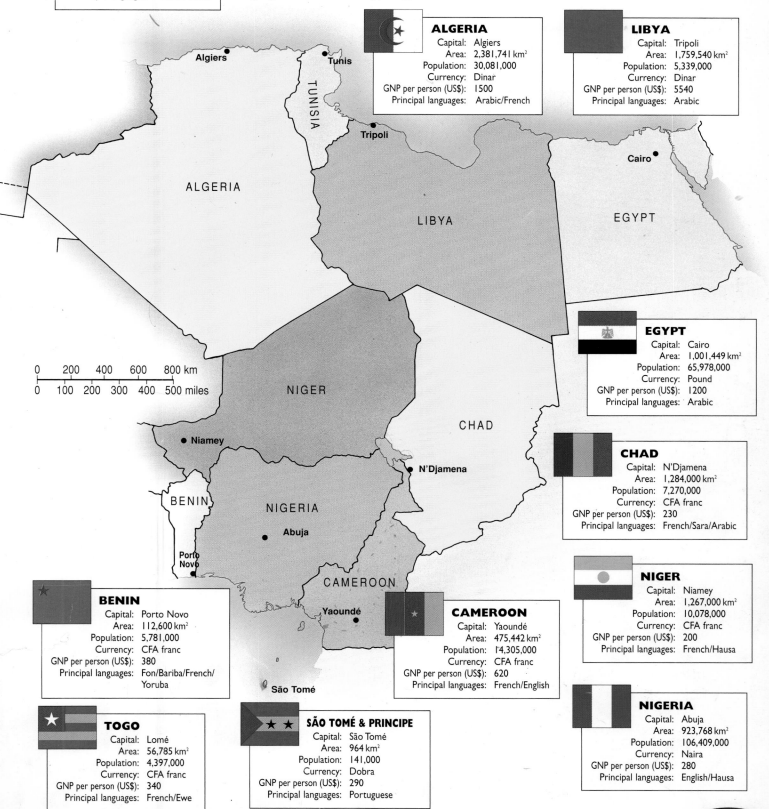

TUNISIA
Capital: Tunis
Area: 163,610 km²
Population: 9,335,000
Currency: Dinar
GNP per person (US$): 2110
Principal languages: Arabic/French

ALGERIA
Capital: Algiers
Area: 2,381,741 km²
Population: 30,081,000
Currency: Dinar
GNP per person (US$): 1500
Principal languages: Arabic/French

LIBYA
Capital: Tripoli
Area: 1,759,540 km²
Population: 5,339,000
Currency: Dinar
GNP per person (US$): 5540
Principal languages: Arabic

EGYPT
Capital: Cairo
Area: 1,001,449 km²
Population: 65,978,000
Currency: Pound
GNP per person (US$): 1200
Principal languages: Arabic

CHAD
Capital: N'Djamena
Area: 1,284,000 km²
Population: 7,270,000
Currency: CFA franc
GNP per person (US$): 230
Principal languages: French/Sara/Arabic

NIGER
Capital: Niamey
Area: 1,267,000 km²
Population: 10,078,000
Currency: CFA franc
GNP per person (US$): 200
Principal languages: French/Hausa

BENIN
Capital: Porto Novo
Area: 112,600 km²
Population: 5,781,000
Currency: CFA franc
GNP per person (US$): 380
Principal languages: Fon/Bariba/French/Yoruba

CAMEROON
Capital: Yaoundé
Area: 475,442 km²
Population: 14,305,000
Currency: CFA franc
GNP per person (US$): 620
Principal languages: French/English

NIGERIA
Capital: Abuja
Area: 923,768 km²
Population: 106,409,000
Currency: Naira
GNP per person (US$): 280
Principal languages: English/Hausa

TOGO
Capital: Lomé
Area: 56,785 km²
Population: 4,397,000
Currency: CFA franc
GNP per person (US$): 340
Principal languages: French/Ewe

SÃO TOMÉ & PRINCIPE
Capital: São Tomé
Area: 964 km²
Population: 141,000
Currency: Dobra
GNP per person (US$): 290
Principal languages: Portuguese

CENTRAL AND EAST AFRICA

Central Africa is an area of great variety. At its heart lies the saucer-shaped basin of the Congo River (also known as the Zaire). Close to the equator, this immense river basin is an area of dense tropical vegetation. Lush vegetation is also widespread in Uganda, Rwanda and Burundi.

The countries of East Africa face the Red Sea or the Indian Ocean. For centuries, many of these countries have had close trade, cultural and religious links with the Arab world. The rearing of livestock – goats, sheep and cattle – is important to the people who live in this part of Africa. There are also large plantations of products such as tea, coffee, cotton and pineapples.

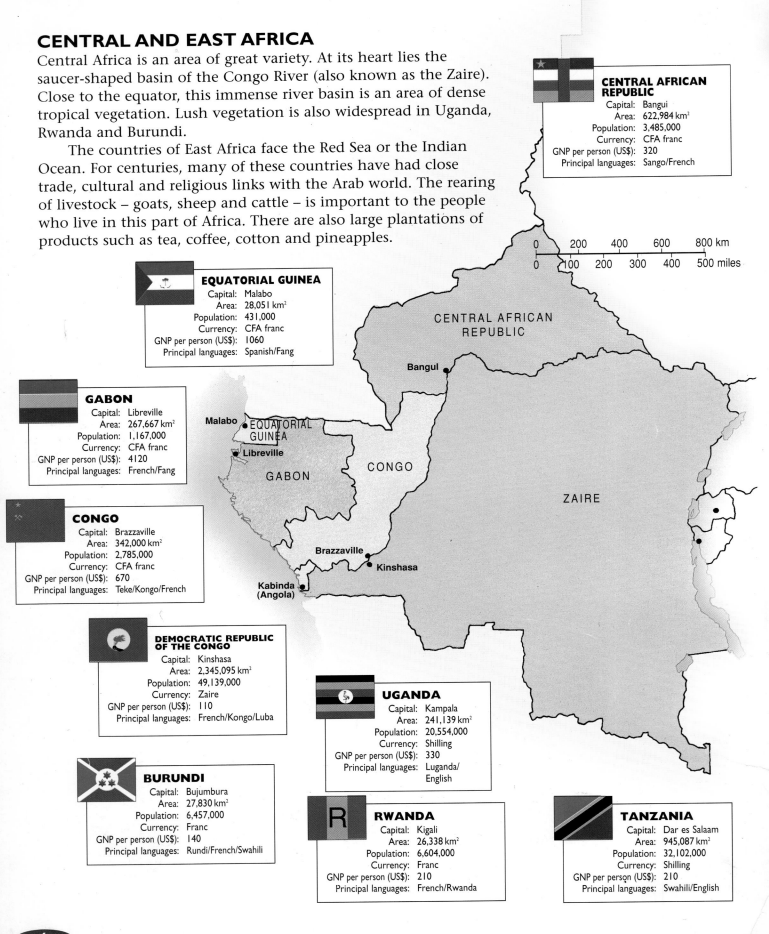

CENTRAL AFRICAN REPUBLIC
Capital: Bangui
Area: 622,984 km²
Population: 3,485,000
Currency: CFA franc
GNP per person (US$): 320
Principal languages: Sango/French

EQUATORIAL GUINEA
Capital: Malabo
Area: 28,051 km²
Population: 431,000
Currency: CFA franc
GNP per person (US$): 1060
Principal languages: Spanish/Fang

GABON
Capital: Libreville
Area: 267,667 km²
Population: 1,167,000
Currency: CFA franc
GNP per person (US$): 4120
Principal languages: French/Fang

CONGO
Capital: Brazzaville
Area: 342,000 km²
Population: 2,785,000
Currency: CFA franc
GNP per person (US$): 670
Principal languages: Teke/Kongo/French

DEMOCRATIC REPUBLIC OF THE CONGO
Capital: Kinshasa
Area: 2,345,095 km²
Population: 49,139,000
Currency: Zaire
GNP per person (US$): 110
Principal languages: French/Kongo/Luba

UGANDA
Capital: Kampala
Area: 241,139 km²
Population: 20,554,000
Currency: Shilling
GNP per person (US$): 330
Principal languages: Luganda/English

BURUNDI
Capital: Bujumbura
Area: 27,830 km²
Population: 6,457,000
Currency: Franc
GNP per person (US$): 140
Principal languages: Rundi/French/Swahili

RWANDA
Capital: Kigali
Area: 26,338 km²
Population: 6,604,000
Currency: Franc
GNP per person (US$): 210
Principal languages: French/Rwanda

TANZANIA
Capital: Dar es Salaam
Area: 945,087 km²
Population: 32,102,000
Currency: Shilling
GNP per person (US$): 210
Principal languages: Swahili/English

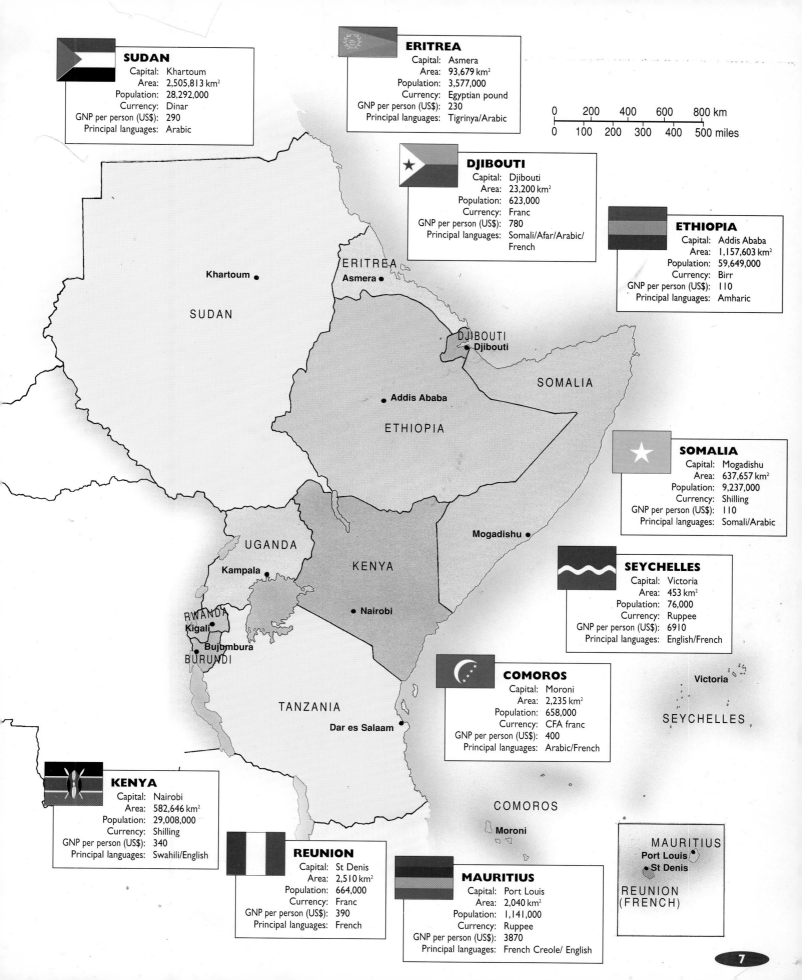

SUDAN
Capital: Khartoum
Area: 2,505,813 km²
Population: 28,292,000
Currency: Dinar
GNP per person (US$): 290
Principal languages: Arabic

ERITREA
Capital: Asmera
Area: 93,679 km²
Population: 3,577,000
Currency: Egyptian pound
GNP per person (US$): 230
Principal languages: Tigrinya/Arabic

DJIBOUTI
Capital: Djibouti
Area: 23,200 km²
Population: 623,000
Currency: Franc
GNP per person (US$): 780
Principal languages: Somali/Afar/Arabic/French

ETHIOPIA
Capital: Addis Ababa
Area: 1,157,603 km²
Population: 59,649,000
Currency: Birr
GNP per person (US$): 110
Principal languages: Amharic

SOMALIA
Capital: Mogadishu
Area: 637,657 km²
Population: 9,237,000
Currency: Shilling
GNP per person (US$): 110
Principal languages: Somali/Arabic

SEYCHELLES
Capital: Victoria
Area: 453 km²
Population: 76,000
Currency: Ruppee
GNP per person (US$): 6910
Principal languages: English/French

COMOROS
Capital: Moroni
Area: 2,235 km²
Population: 658,000
Currency: CFA franc
GNP per person (US$): 400
Principal languages: Arabic/French

KENYA
Capital: Nairobi
Area: 582,646 km²
Population: 29,008,000
Currency: Shilling
GNP per person (US$): 340
Principal languages: Swahili/English

REUNION
Capital: St Denis
Area: 2,510 km²
Population: 664,000
Currency: Franc
GNP per person (US$): 390
Principal languages: French

MAURITIUS
Capital: Port Louis
Area: 2,040 km²
Population: 1,141,000
Currency: Ruppee
GNP per person (US$): 3870
Principal languages: French Creole/ English

Scale:
0   200   400   600   800 km
0 100 200 300 400 500 miles

Map labels:
Khartoum
SUDAN
ERITREA
Asmera
DJIBOUTI
Djibouti
SOMALIA
Addis Ababa
ETHIOPIA
Mogadishu
UGANDA
Kampala
KENYA
RWANDA
Kigali
Bujumbura
BURUNDI
Nairobi
TANZANIA
Dar es Salaam
Victoria
SEYCHELLES
COMOROS
Moroni
MAURITIUS
Port Louis
St Denis
REUNION (FRENCH)

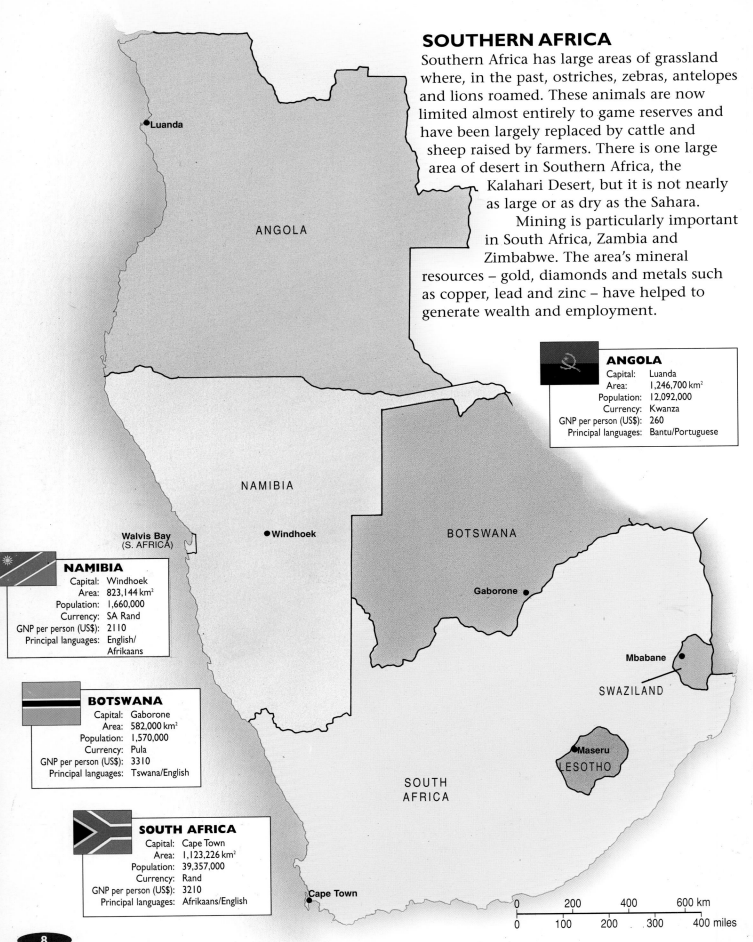

SOUTHERN AFRICA

Southern Africa has large areas of grassland where, in the past, ostriches, zebras, antelopes and lions roamed. These animals are now limited almost entirely to game reserves and have been largely replaced by cattle and sheep raised by farmers. There is one large area of desert in Southern Africa, the Kalahari Desert, but it is not nearly as large or as dry as the Sahara.

Mining is particularly important in South Africa, Zambia and Zimbabwe. The area's mineral resources – gold, diamonds and metals such as copper, lead and zinc – have helped to generate wealth and employment.

ANGOLA
Capital: Luanda
Area: 1,246,700 km²
Population: 12,092,000
Currency: Kwanza
GNP per person (US$): 260
Principal languages: Bantu/Portuguese

NAMIBIA
Capital: Windhoek
Area: 823,144 km²
Population: 1,660,000
Currency: SA Rand
GNP per person (US$): 2110
Principal languages: English/Afrikaans

BOTSWANA
Capital: Gaborone
Area: 582,000 km²
Population: 1,570,000
Currency: Pula
GNP per person (US$): 3310
Principal languages: Tswana/English

SOUTH AFRICA
Capital: Cape Town
Area: 1,123,226 km²
Population: 39,357,000
Currency: Rand
GNP per person (US$): 3210
Principal languages: Afrikaans/English

ANGOLA

•Luanda

NAMIBIA

•Windhoek

Walvis Bay
(S. AFRICA)

BOTSWANA

Gaborone•

SOUTH
AFRICA

•Mbabane

SWAZILAND

•Maseru

LESOTHO

•Cape Town

0	200	400	600 km

0	100	200	300	400 miles

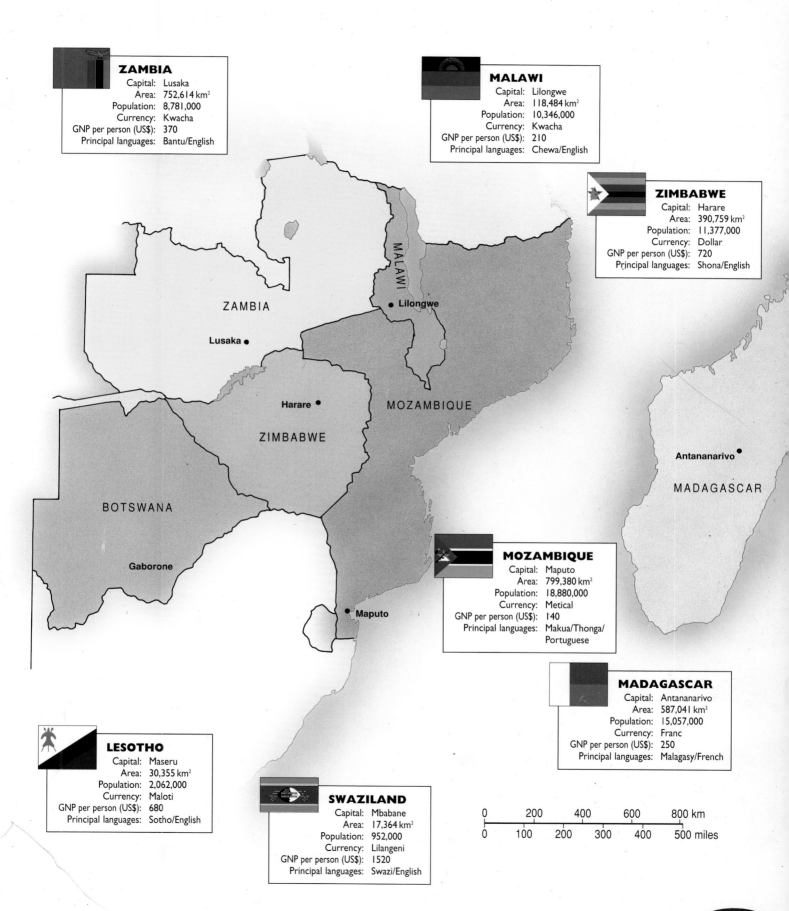

ZAMBIA
Capital: Lusaka
Area: 752,614 km²
Population: 8,781,000
Currency: Kwacha
GNP per person (US$): 370
Principal languages: Bantu/English

MALAWI
Capital: Lilongwe
Area: 118,484 km²
Population: 10,346,000
Currency: Kwacha
GNP per person (US$): 210
Principal languages: Chewa/English

ZIMBABWE
Capital: Harare
Area: 390,759 km²
Population: 11,377,000
Currency: Dollar
GNP per person (US$): 720
Principal languages: Shona/English

MOZAMBIQUE
Capital: Maputo
Area: 799,380 km²
Population: 18,880,000
Currency: Metical
GNP per person (US$): 140
Principal languages: Makua/Thonga/
Portuguese

MADAGASCAR
Capital: Antananarivo
Area: 587,041 km²
Population: 15,057,000
Currency: Franc
GNP per person (US$): 250
Principal languages: Malagasy/French

LESOTHO
Capital: Maseru
Area: 30,355 km²
Population: 2,062,000
Currency: Maloti
GNP per person (US$): 680
Principal languages: Sotho/English

SWAZILAND
Capital: Mbabane
Area: 17,364 km²
Population: 952,000
Currency: Lilangeni
GNP per person (US$): 1520
Principal languages: Swazi/English

ZAMBIA

MALAWI

Lilongwe

Lusaka

Harare

ZIMBABWE

MOZAMBIQUE

BOTSWANA

Gaborone

Maputo

MADAGASCAR

Antananarivo

| 0 | 200 | 400 | 600 | 800 km |
| 0 | 100 | 200 | 300 | 400 | 500 miles |

INTRODUCTION

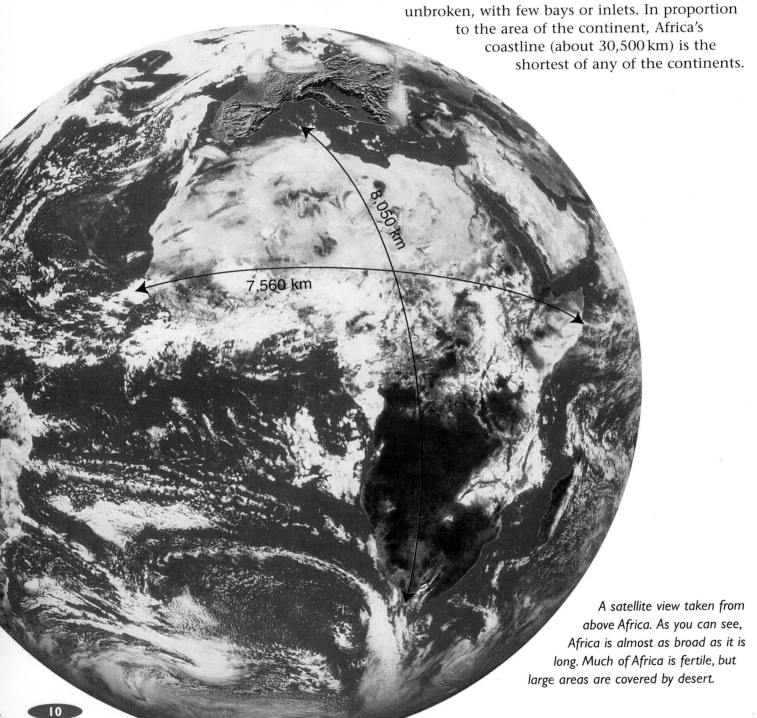

Africa covers more than one-fifth of the earth's land surface. It has an area of some 30,330,000 km², which makes it the second largest of the seven continents.

The Mediterranean Sea lies to the north of Africa, separating it from Europe. The narrow Red Sea lies to the northeast, separating Africa from Asia. To the east of Africa lies the Indian Ocean, while the Atlantic Ocean lies to the west. The African coastline is relatively unbroken, with few bays or inlets. In proportion to the area of the continent, Africa's coastline (about 30,500 km) is the shortest of any of the continents.

8,050 km

7,560 km

A satellite view taken from above Africa. As you can see, Africa is almost as broad as it is long. Much of Africa is fertile, but large areas are covered by desert.

Left *The lands close to the equator are covered with dense rain forests. In West Africa they spread inland from the Gulf of Guinea. The hot, wet climate encourages growth of dense vegetation, which supports a huge variety of wildlife.*

TROPIC OF CANCER

EQUATOR

TROPIC OF CAPRICORN

The equator is an imaginary circle running right around the world. We use it as the base line for measuring latitude north or south. The line runs right through the middle of Africa: a large part of the continent is in the Northern Hemisphere, while the rest is in the Southern Hemisphere. Countries which are in the region of 10° latitude north or south of the equator are called equatorial lands.

Above *The equator runs through the middle of Africa.*

Below *The globe 50 million years ago.*

If we look at a map or globe, one of the most interesting features is the way South America and Africa seem to fit together. Without too much difficulty, southern Australia and Antarctica can also be put together. Geologists have also discovered that similar rocks occur in, for example, Brazil and southwest Africa, and also certain plants and reptiles. Evidence such as this indicates that these continents were joined together from about 50–100 million years ago, after which they began to spread apart.

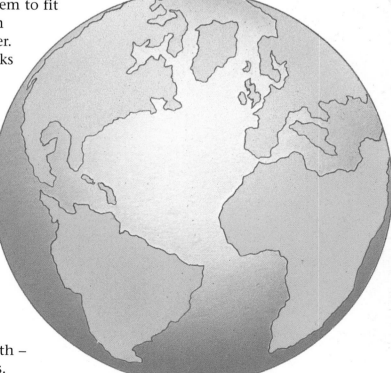

Africa today is a continent of contrasts. The media presents us with a picture of poverty, war and famine, but there are many other views of Africa. The continent is rich in resources and in the diversity of its people, and many real achievements have been made in the past 100 years. Africa is similar to other continents in some of the choices it faces – development, environmental challenges and population growth – but different in its history, traditions and values.

THE GEOGRAPHY OF AFRICA

MOUNTAINS

Much of Africa is 300–700 m above sea-level. From a narrow, low-lying coastal strip, the land rises to a great rolling plateau, with the highest parts in East Africa, including the Ethiopian and Kenyan highlands. Many of these highland areas were the sites of the earliest African kingdoms. Only in later years, did people begin to settle in large numbers along the coastal strip, where today some of the highest concentrations of people are located.

Over the millions of years following the break-up of the continents, the structure and shape of Africa as we know it today began to emerge. Due to continued movement in the earth's core, the plates that underlie the surface continue spreading and can cause tremendous pressure, leading to folding and uplifting, creating mountain ranges and valleys.

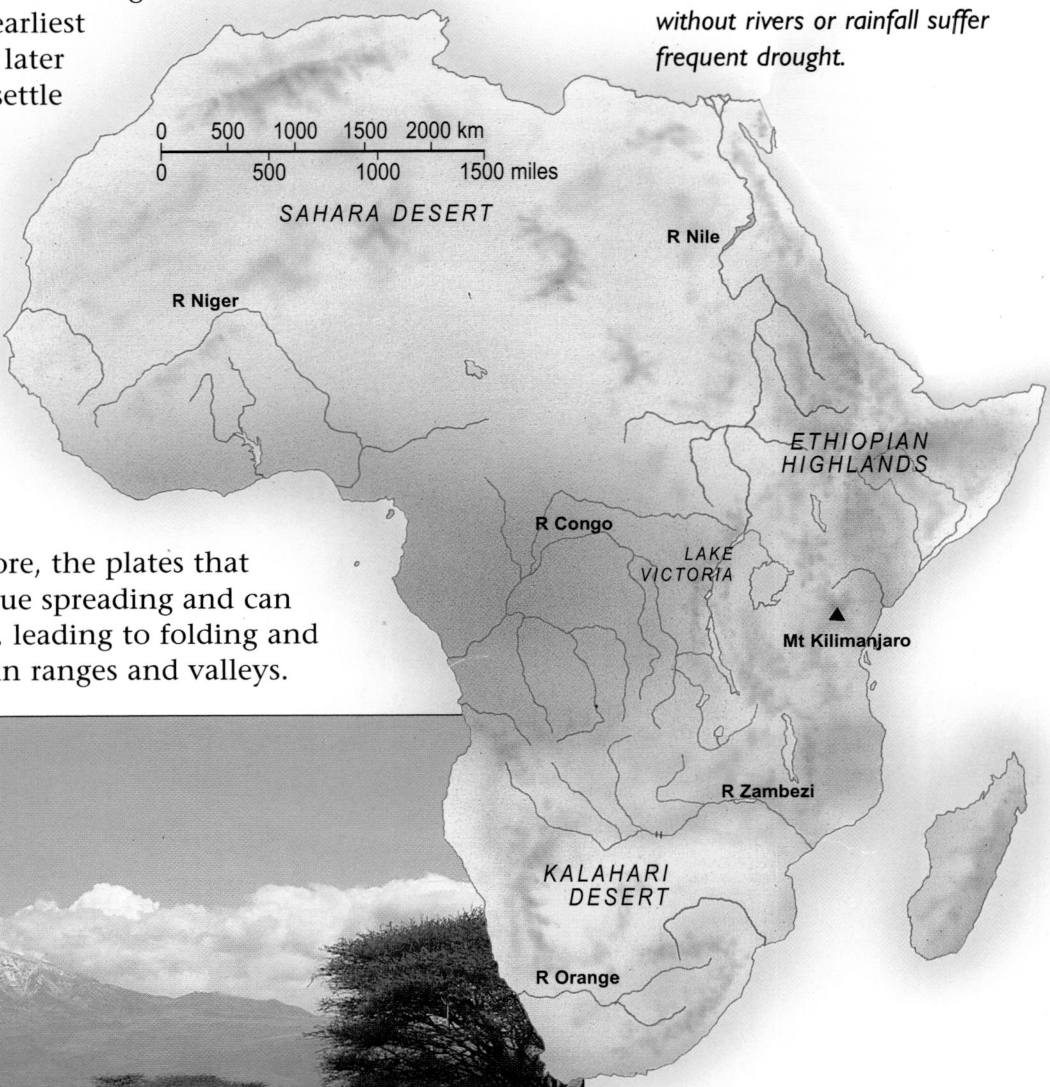

This map shows the variety of natural features to be found in Africa. Large rivers feed fertile plains as they bring water from the mountains. Other areas without rivers or rainfall suffer frequent drought.

| 0 | 500 | 1000 | 1500 | 2000 km |
| 0 | | 500 | 1000 | 1500 miles |

SAHARA DESERT

R Nile

R Niger

ETHIOPIAN HIGHLANDS

R Congo

LAKE VICTORIA

▲ Mt Kilimanjaro

R Zambezi

KALAHARI DESERT

R Orange

Mount Kilimanjaro in Tanzania, close to the border with Kenya, is 5,895 m high – the highest mountain in Africa. Although it is situated close to the equator, the peak is permanently covered with snow. Lower down the mountain there are forests and grassland then, further down, the slopes are intensely cultivated.

A great valley, known as the Rift Valley, cuts through East Africa from north to south. This valley contains some of Africa's biggest lakes – Albert, Malawi, Turkana and Tanganyika. These lakes help feed the River Nile, the River Congo and the River Zambesi. This is Lake Bogoria.

RIVERS AND LAKES

Rivers have attacked the African landscape for millions of years, gouging away deep and spectacular valleys and gorges. Africa's major rivers include the Nile, the Congo, the Niger, the Zambezi and the Orange (also known as the Garib). Rapids and falls make these rivers difficult to navigate, but offer tremendous possibilities for harnessing hydroelectric power. It has been estimated that Africa holds about 40 per cent of the earth's hydroelectric power potential.

The River Nile rises in Burundi and flows into the Mediterranean Sea near Alexandria in Egypt. Its total length has been calculated as 6,650 km. Nine countries share its waters which bring life to surrounding lands.

DESERTS

In Africa, as in other parts of the world, land is one of the most precious resources. But in parts of Africa, valuable agricultural land is in danger of turning into desert. A large part of North Africa, from the West African Sahel to Somalia, is under threat of desertification. Geographers call these dry, parched areas 'arid' or 'semi-arid'.

In recent decades, there has been great variation in the amount of rain that has fallen on this southern edge of the Sahara Desert. In the 1950s and 1960s there was above-average rainfall in most years. Crops grew well and animal herds thrived. In the 1970s and 1980s, however, rainfall was well below average. Crops failed, animals died and people suffered from famine during the most severe drought of the twentieth century.

The Sahara Desert is gradually extending even further to the south. Some scientists say that the abuse of the environment has stripped the earth of the natural protection that would prevent it from turning into desert. Others believe that what is now happening in the Sahel is part of a natural process that has been happening for thousands of years.

The Sahara Desert is the largest desert in the world, stretching from the Atlantic Ocean right across northern Africa to the Red Sea. It covers one quarter of Africa's land surface – measuring 5,000 km from east to west and extending 1,500 km from the Mediterranean coastal plain in the north to the Sahel in the south.

LIVING IN AN ARID AREA

Messoud Ould Jiddou describes the situation in the Sahel like this. 'When my parents were young, there was enough rainfall in most years to feed the crops and to fill the wells. Now there are more people sharing the land.

'My mother says that she has to go much farther to find firewood for cooking than was the case in the past. In many areas, there are scarcely any trees left and the land has no shelter from the heat of the sun or the force of the winds. My father says that the land is becoming poorer year by year. The topsoil is being eroded, trees are disappearing and the remaining vegetation is being eaten by the animals.

'Because it is so hard for people to survive in our area, some of our people have gone to work on larger farms and some have gone to look for work in distant towns.

'Now, even during the wet season, we can't be sure of adequate rainfall.

'Sometimes, at the beginning or end of the rainy season, great thunderstorms bring lots of rain. Because the torrential rain may fall close to one village and not to another, we have to be ready to move with our herds of cattle, sheep, goats or camels.

'The government says that we should stay in our own area, but that is impossible if we are to survive. The farmers who have planted crops can only hope and pray that the rains will fall in their area.

'Many people depend on receiving grain from aid organizations to survive, but we need long-term solutions. In my area, the people of the village are advising an aid agency, which is helping us to plant a new forest.

'We protect the young plants from the animals because we know that in the future they will give us fruit, firewood and protection from the sun and wind.'

THE WEATHER

Africa's location gives the continent a varied climate. The wettest parts are around the equator, where the sun evaporates large amounts of moisture from the sea and land, and this condenses into clouds. As the clouds rise, they shed their moisture as rain. In the areas to the north and south of the equator, this process is less reliable and there are large areas of arid land – the Kalahari Desert in the south and the Sahara in the north.

This climatic pattern affects the vegetation of the continent, and the prospects for farming. The rainforest areas around the equator, when cleared, are suitable for a wide variety of crops such as cocoa, oil palm, bananas, cassava and yams. The sub-humid lands to the south of the rain forests are covered with open woodland and savanna grassland. There is a rainy season of between 4–8 months, which allows cereals such as maize and sorghum to be widely cultivated. The arid areas are dominated by grassland, with sparse cover of trees and shrubs, and very little rainfall. The main crop is millet.

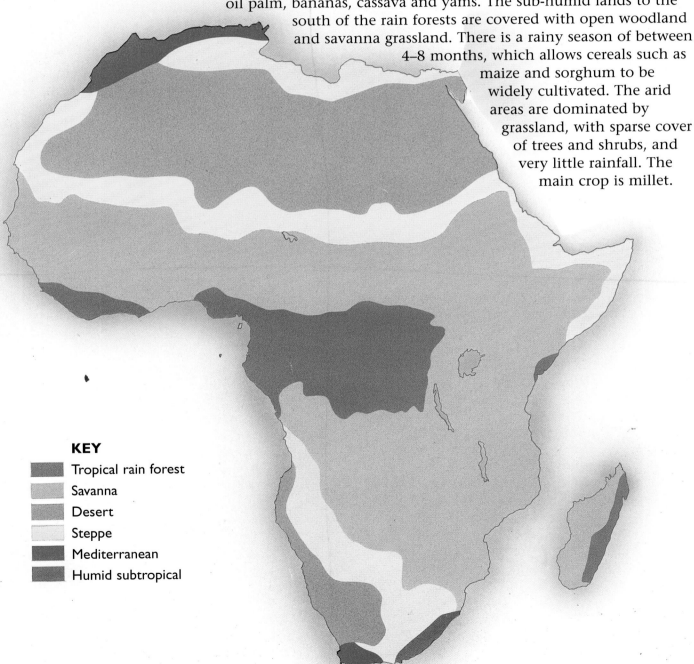

KEY

- Tropical rain forest
- Savanna
- Desert
- Steppe
- Mediterranean
- Humid subtropical

The Tropics

At midday, the sun is very high in the African sky. In central Africa it is often almost directly overhead at noon. You might expect that the sun would shine directly down on the equator every day of the year. And so it would, but for the fact that the earth's axis is tilted at 23.45°. Because of this, the North Pole is tilted towards the sun for one part of the year, bringing warmer weather to northern latitudes. During this time, the sun's rays shine directly down on the lands to the north of the equator.

Towards the end of June, the midday sun shines directly on the Tropic of Cancer, which is 23.45° north of the equator. By the end of December, however, the midday sun is shining directly down on places that are on the Tropic of Capricorn, 23.45° south of the equator. Places that are between 23.45° north or south of the equator are said to be in the tropics. We call these tropical lands.

Above *A man picking tea in Kenya. Parts of the Kenyan highlands have regular rainfall and are particularly suitable for growing tea. Nairobi, one of Kenya's biggest cities, is also located on a high plateau, which gives it a pleasant climate. Other parts of Kenya are entirely arid.*

Tropic of Cancer

equator

Tropic of Capricorn

Inset *This figure shows the position of Africa in relation to the equator and the Tropic of Capricorn and the Tropic of Cancer.*

Left *Each year, in June, the Nile begins to flood over the surrounding lands, making them suitable for agriculture. For centuries, the Egyptians have used a network of canals and ditches to increase the irrigated areas, but the floodwaters are available for only a short period of time. This photograph shows an archimedean screw being used to pump water to the fields where various crops are grown.*

THE HISTORY OF AFRICA

Most scientists now agree that Africa was the birthplace of the human race. Archaeologists have found bones in Kenya and other parts of East Africa that are almost 5 million years old. The first inhabitants hunted, gathered and fished for their food. Then in about 4000 BC settlements grew up in Egypt along the banks of the River Nile. By 2000 BC, these early settlers had learned how to make iron tools and weapons, and had spread westwards and southwards. Trade became very important, with Africa supplying gold, slaves, precious stones, ivory, feathers, hides and animals to Europe, China and other parts of Asia.

Before Europeans arrived in Africa, the continent was dominated by a number of kingdoms. Small trading villages grew up along the east coast and traded with countries along the Indian Ocean coast, especially Arabia. There were other early African kingdoms in the interior. As far back as AD 1000, people from the north established rich kingdoms in Zimbabwe. These lasted until they were attacked and destroyed by Bantu peoples from South Africa. The area was then taken over and ruled by Europeans. Other powerful states included the Luba and Lunda peoples in what is now the Congo and Angola, and the Zulus of South Africa.

The three most famous and powerful kingdoms were those of Ghana (500–1000 AD), Mali (1200–1400 AD) and Songhai (1400–1500 AD). They grew wealthy from the trans-Saharan trade routes and developed strong trading links with the Arab merchants of North and East Africa and the Middle East.

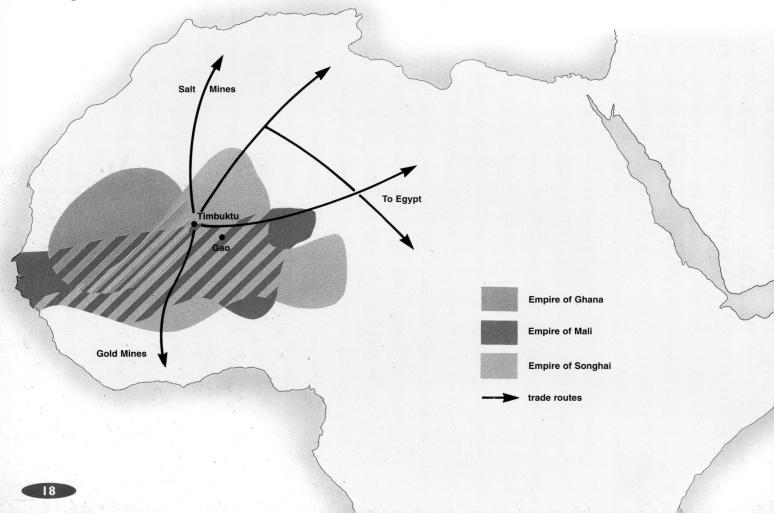

Salt Mines

To Egypt

Timbuktu

Gao

Gold Mines

Empire of Ghana

Empire of Mali

Empire of Songhai

→ trade routes

Above The camel, the 'ship of the desert', was probably first introduced into Africa by the Romans. The camel, which can go long distances without a drink, was ideally suited to the trans-Saharan trade routes so vital to the early wealth of North Africa.

Left About AD 1200, people from Arabia moved to the islands off Africa's east coast and established rich city states. The most famous of these were Sofala, Pemba, Mogadishu and Mozambique. These cities declined in the sixteenth century after attacks from Portuguese sea captains. The Portuguese then took over the lucrative East African trade.

Below Dhows travelled regularly along and across the Indian Ocean supplying markets and traders. In some places there were specific market days set aside. Metal bars were used as money.

COLONIALISM

By the middle of the sixteenth century, other European countries began to challenge the Portuguese for the profitable East African trade. During the 1800s, European explorers travelled through Africa and soon the European nations controlled large parts of the continent. By the beginning of the 1900s, virtually all of Africa, except Ethiopia and Liberia, was divided up into colonies by the dominant European powers – Belgium, Britain, France, Germany, Italy and Portugal. The colonies helped to provide money and resources for the rapid development of Europe. Much of this was achieved at the expense of Africa and the Africans.

The colonial period laid the foundations of many of Africa's current problems. The boundary lines of states frequently divided up tribal groups or their traditional lands, ignoring local geography and the importance of access to water or to resources. This often led to conflict over boundaries, land or resources, and has contributed to political instability in many modern African states. Land was taken from local people to grow crops that were needed in Europe. Local industries were not developed if they competed with those of the colonial powers. Large parts of many of the cities which grew up were often reserved for white élites.

This old print shows two British explorers, Richard Burton and John Hanning Speke, being received at a king's court in Central Africa. The two men set off in 1857 to find the source of the River Nile, and Speke gave Lake Victoria its name.

The colonial powers introduced their own cultures, languages and religions into the colonies. In schools, education was geared towards producing civil servants needed for administering the colony rather than towards educating all local people for their own development and that of their country. People in Europe were encouraged to see Africans as lazy, ignorant, often violent or barbaric, lacking in development or education and generally unsophisticated. Many of these false attitudes and viewpoints have continued through to today.

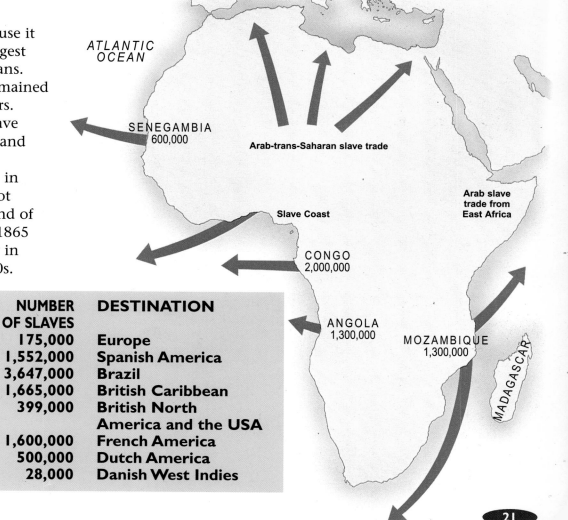

Above Trade between the USA (The New World), Europe and Africa formed a triangle.

THE SLAVE TRADE

Long before the slave trade to the New World began, Arab traders shipped African slaves to India, Indonesia, Egypt, Turkey and Persia. By the mid-1500s the slave trade had grown enormously, to provide labour for the sugar and tobacco plantations of the New World. The slave trade had enormous influence on the later development of Africa because it removed many of the youngest and most able-bodied Africans. The population of Africa remained stagnant for nearly 200 years.

The profits from the slave trade, as well as the misery and suffering it caused, were enormous. It became illegal in England in 1772, but did not finally end until after the end of the American Civil War in 1865 and the abolition of slavery in Cuba and Brazil in the 1880s.

Right The map shows principal sources and destinations of slaves, 1526–1870, showing the number of slaves leaving each area.

NUMBER OF SLAVES	DESTINATION
175,000	Europe
1,552,000	Spanish America
3,647,000	Brazil
1,665,000	British Caribbean
399,000	British North America and the USA
1,600,000	French America
500,000	Dutch America
28,000	Danish West Indies

INDEPENDENCE AND DEMOCRACY

In some countries, such as South Africa and Zambia, independence was won without the use of violence. In other countries, such as Algeria and Kenya, there was a long struggle between liberation armies and the military forces of colonial powers. Some countries, such as Angola and Zaire, suffered civil war as opposing forces tried to take control from the colonial powers.

Many African states have had little experience of democracy. In some parts of Africa, the traditional experience of leadership was of tribal groupings led by a powerful king or chieftain. When African people began to band together to fight for their independence, they usually formed a common opposition to the colonial powers. Then, when independence was won, these groups took control. But very often there was no internal opposition in the country, so it often took many years before other opposition parties emerged. For this reason, many African states have had years of one party rule.

THE GAMBIA (1965)
MAURITANIA (1960)
MALI (1960)
NIGER (1960)
SENEGAL (1960)
UPPER VOLTA (1960)
GUINEA (1958)
IVORY COAST (1960)
GHANA (1957)
NIGERIA (1960)
CHAD (1960)
SUDAN (1956)
DJIBOUTI (1977)
SOMALIA (1960)
SIERRA LEONE (1961)
BENIN (1960)
GUINEA-BISSAU (1974)
TOGO (1960)
CAMEROON (1960)
CENTRAL AFRICAN EMPIRE (1960)
GABON (1960)
CONGO (1960)
ZAIRE (1960)
UGANDA (1962)
KENYA (1963)
RWANDA (1962)
BURUNDI (1962)
TANZANIA (1964)
EQUATORIAL GUINEA (1968)
ANGOLA (1975)
ZAMBIA (1964)
MALAWI (1964)
COMORU ISLANDS (1975)
RHODESIA (1965)
MOZAMBIQUE (1975)
MALAGASY REPUBLIC (MADAGASCAR) (1960)
BOTSWANA (1966)
SWAZILAND (1968)
SOUTH AFRICA (1931)
LESOTHO (1966)

Independence from

- Britain
- Britain and Egypt
- Italy and Britain
- France
- Portugal
- Belgium
- Spain

Right *The borders of many African states have their origins in the colonial period. In some cases, different tribal groupings share a common state, and this has led to bitter fighting. In Rwanda, for example, large numbers of Tutsi were massacred by the Hutu in 1993 and 1994. Here the Rwandese Patriotic Front demonstrate in Kigali.*

In this situation, it has often been possible for a party leader to ignore the rules about elections. Some people who were democratically elected have continued in office as dictators, denying the people their political rights. In other instances, army leaders have ignored democratic procedures and seized power and control.

While there are many challenges to democracy in Africa, there are also signs of hope. People are organizing themselves to build schools for their children and to develop irrigation and water schemes. Local groups are replanting the forests and taking action to protect Africa's wildlife heritage. In some places, people are opposing undemocratic regimes and demanding political rights.

Many international organizations and aid agencies provide support to such initiatives, in the belief that such efforts are the foundation on which Africa's democratic future depends. The Organisation of African Unity (OAU) aims to promote friendship and cooperation between African states. The African Economic Community (AEC), based on the model of the European Economic Community, was set up in 1994.

RESOURCES

FOOD AND FARMING

Agriculture is vitally important in Africa because 70 per cent of the population depend upon it for a living. However, only one-fifth of the land surface is suitable for farming, and much of that is seriously deficient in the minerals that are vital for plant growth. Drought also affects large parts of the continent. Lack of technology means that only 3 per cent of African land is irrigated, and of that 70 per cent is in only three countries – Nigeria, Sudan and Madagascar.

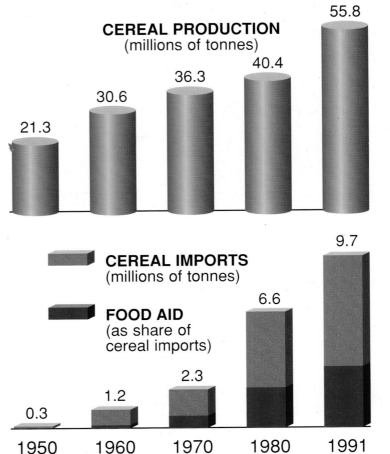

CEREAL PRODUCTION (millions of tonnes)

21.3   30.6   36.3   40.4   55.8

CEREAL IMPORTS (millions of tonnes)

FOOD AID (as share of cereal imports)

0.3   1.2   2.3   6.6   9.7

1950   1960   1970   1980   1991

Above While food production in Africa is increasing, it is not keeping pace with population growth and Africa has become more dependent on external aid.

Above About 60 per cent of the world's cocoa is grown in Africa. Other export crops are coffee and tea, and various fruits from North Africa. Palm oil and vegetable oil are also produced in large amounts.

Right Daily calorie supply for some African countries. The first column shows average daily calorie intake per capita. The other columns show the per capita daily intake as a percentage of the developed world average.

Country	Daily calorie supply (1992)	Daily calorie supply per capita (developed world = 100)	
		1965	1992
Sierra Leone	1,695	64	54
Ethiopia	1,610	62	51
Mozambique	1,680	69	54
Chad	1,989	80	64
Uganda	2,162	77	69
Mauritania	2,685	71	86
Nigeria	2,125	77	68
Sudan	2,202	64	70
Ghana	2,206	70	71
Morocco	2,985	74	95
Gabon	2,511	65	80
Egypt	3,336	78	100+
Libya	3,310	67	100+

Source: **UNDP (1995)** *Human Development Report.* **Oxford University Press.**

There are three major types of farm in Africa. The majority of farmers live on very small 'subsistence' farms, depending on family labour to produce food and rear livestock. Many of them also produce small quantities of crops for the export market. Second, there is a growing but still small group of middle-sized farms using hired labour, and sometimes machines, to produce food for local markets and for export. Third, there is a small number of large estate farms, or plantations, which use machinery and hired labour to produce 'cash crops' mostly for export. These farms are often found in countries that have a colonial past, such as Zaire, Zimbabwe, Kenya and Zambia.

There has also been an emergence of rich African 'telephone farmers' who do not actually live on their farms (and run them by telephone), and of large-scale export-orientated farming, or agribusiness.

In recent years many African governments have concentrated on export farming and have neglected the needs of smaller farmers. The use of fertilizer is the lowest in the world, and up to 40 per cent of crops can be lost to pests, weeds and diseases. Although tractor use increased by 20 per cent in the 1980s, it is still only 4 per cent of the European level. Today, with a rapidly growing population, most experts agree that greater attention needs to be paid to Africa's millions of subsistence farmers.

Below *Percentage of agricultural work done by men and women in Africa.*

Men

Women

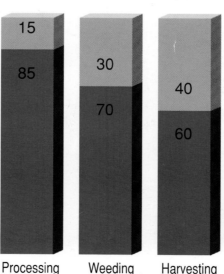

15	30	40	50	50	70
85	70	60	50	50	30
Processing and storing crops	Weeding	Harvesting	Caring for livestock	Planting	Ploughing

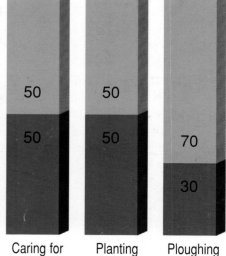

INDUSTRY

Africa has some of the largest mineral deposits in the world, but many African countries lack the ability to refine the raw materials they produce. In the past, the colonial powers saw Africa as a producer of raw materials to meet their own requirements. There was little need to develop African industry, other than a basic processing of metal ores to make them more easily transportable.

Today, most African countries continue to export mineral resources, which are relatively cheap, and to import mostly manufactured goods, which are relatively expensive – thus receiving far less for the type of goods they produce than they pay for the goods they purchase. Some countries are very dependent on two or three export commodities and, in a year when prices for these goods drop, they have severe financial problems.

When Africa earns less, it can buy less. In recent decades, Africa's share of world trade has become smaller. Programmes of healthcare, education and the provision of safe water have come under threat as more and more of Africa's earnings are used to pay the debts that African countries owe to more developed and wealthier countries.

Above In recent years, a number of large motor manufacturers have set up assembly plants in African countries. Kits containing the parts, such as engine, chassis and axles, are imported. The final assembly work is done in Africa, giving employment to local people.

MINERAL RESOURCES

- **South Africa contains one of the world's seven major uranium reserves.**
- **West Africa is a major world supplier of iron ore.**
- **Great Dyke in Zimbabwe and other African locations together produce almost all the world's chromium.**
- **Africa supplies one-third of the world's bauxite.**
- **Half the world's supply of gold that is still underground is located in South Africa.**
- **South Africa and Namibia have large reserves of gem diamonds.**
- **Libya and Nigeria are major world exporters of oil.**
- **The eight biggest mineral producers obtained 29.4 per cent of their GDP from mining in 1989.**
- **Ten per cent of the GDP of the whole of Africa came from mining in 1989.**

Guinea has the biggest reserves of bauxite, which is used to make aluminium, in the world. But there are few processing plants, so instead of selling expensive aluminium, Guinea sells unprocessed bauxite at a lower price.

COPPER MINING IN ZAMBIA

Tambala Tschombe remembers the story of his family's work for the mining industry. 'In 1948, my grandparents moved to Nkana, where my grandfather was given a job and a regular salary by a mining company. At that time, all the bosses were well-paid Europeans.

'When our country gained independence and became known as Zambia in 1964, there were six large mines here. They were owned by two British companies and employed more than 45,000 workers. Copper was almost the only export of Zambia – making up 97 per cent of our export earnings. By then, my father was also working in the mine. He says that this was a very difficult time for workers, with a lot of trouble and strikes in the mines. When the Europeans left, their work was done by Africans, but the companies didn't want to pay them as much as they had paid the European workers. Finally, our government took control of the mines.

'During the 1960s and early 1970s, there were very good prices for copper on the international market. But from 1975 to 1986, the prices fell. This was a disaster – many workers lost their jobs. It was also very difficult for our country, as we could buy much less from other countries with the money we earned from selling copper. Although the price of copper has improved since the 1980s, it will be a long time before our country really benefits from the wealth of its natural resources.'

TOURISM

Tourists in search of something different are attracted by the strength of traditional African cultures and ways of living. For the local people, tourism has advantages and disadvantages.

ADVANTAGES	DISADVANTAGES
It brings valuable currency earnings.	It increases inequality between areas by promoting islands of development.
It provides employment.	Jobs are often menial service jobs.
It helps to promote knowledge of Africa.	Local culture is often seen as strange.
It helps to protect wildlife.	It can also lead to damage to aspects of the environment other than animals, eg. vegetation and management of the land.

Above The copper industry is based in a part of Africa known as the Copperbelt, which stretches across Zambia and into Zaire. Copper is the second most widely used metal in the world. It is used in electrical cables and in electronic and communications equipment. Copper is also found in Kenya, Mauritania and Mozambique.

Right Big game hunters have been almost entirely replaced by camera-carrying tourists. In the safari parks wild animals can be seen in their natural habitat.

THE PEOPLES OF AFRICA

RELIGION

The distribution of religions in Africa today tells us a lot about the past. Almost all of North Africa and many of the eastern coastal areas, especially the towns and cities, are predominantly Muslim, which clearly reflects the Arab influence. Much of Africa south of the Sahara is dominated by traditional African religions and by Christianity. These two religious traditions relate to Africa's colonial past.

It is very difficult to be precise about the percentage of Africans of each religion. The number of Christians is estimated at roughly 44 per cent of the total population. The number rises to 53 per cent if we include only those states in sub-Saharan Africa. The number of Muslims is estimated at 41 per cent overall, and 29 per cent for sub-Saharan Africa. It is estimated that by the year 2000, these two major religions will have about 300 million followers each.

On a day-to-day basis, Muslims and Christians live peacefully together. However, in some countries, political disputes sometimes become disputes between the two religions and this can result in violent conflicts. This is the case, for example, in Sudan and Nigeria, where conflicts over land, resources and political power have strong religious overtones.

Islam

Islam came to North Africa from Arabia in the seventh century. From the urban areas it spread along the Mediterranean coast to Spain. By the eleventh century, it had spread further south into the Sahel region and beyond. Islam remained largely static until the nineteenth century, when it experienced a surge of growth in East Africa, spreading into Somalia and further along the eastern coast. The greatest growth has been in the last 100 years.

These Muslims are worshipping in a Cairo mosque.

Christianity

Christianity was established in Africa in the first century AD. It spread from the Holy Land to Egypt, along the north coast and then further south into Ethiopia. The Coptic Church in Ethiopia was ruled not from Rome, but from Alexandria in Egypt. Christianity's first major phase of growth came with the arrival of the Portuguese in the fifteenth and sixteenth centuries. During this period it spread along the east coast and down into South Africa. In the eighteenth century, Protestantism spread to the west and south. The missionaries who organized this expansion also became involved in health and educational work. Phase three of the spread of Christianity came in the nineteenth century, when it spread inland from the coastal areas. During this phase, independent African Christian churches also appeared. Because of the close links between Christianity and colonialism in Africa's history many Africans believe it is still a colonial church.

Above *Archbishop Desmond Tutu in South Africa.*

In recent decades, especially since the end of the Second World War, a great variety of new Christian churches – particularly international evangelical churches and the Jehovah's Witnesses – have become active in Africa. As is the case with the older Christian churches, their activities have been the focus of much debate, particularly as to how they relate to Africa's traditional religions.

Traditional religions

Traditional religions are closely linked to local cultures. They play an important role in helping people to understand forces that they can't control or fully understand, and relate to specific needs – such as the need for a good harvest, rain or the birth of healthy children.

Below *The shrine of the Oshun goddess at Oshogbo, Nigeria.*

Traditional religions believe in a creator who is usually male, but there are some female gods. Many of the gods are thought to be ancestors living in the ground, or in some far distant place. Their job is to look after the interests of the living. As in most other religions, there is a priest class and there are often other important figures such as rainmakers and sorcerers. Today many Africans blend elements of both traditional and other religions together.

POPULATION

The map on this page gives a general picture of where the largest numbers of people live in Africa. Many people live along the coast of North Africa, especially in Egypt, Tunisia and Morocco and in the capital cities. There are heavy concentrations of population in the states of West Africa, particularly in Nigeria and Ghana. The east coast is also heavily settled from Ethiopia in the north through Kenya and Tanzania to South Africa.

The most striking aspect of population growth in Africa, as in many other parts of the developing world in the past two decades, has been the move from the countryside to the cities. Today, most of the world's fastest-growing cities are in Africa, and a great many of the new urban dwellers live in slum areas.

People leave rural areas because of poverty, poor job prospects, lower wages, fewer schools, fewer doctors and hospitals and poorer services (eg. water and sanitation).

People migrate to cities because of job opportunities, higher wages, better schools, more doctors and hospitals, better services and a better social life.

Many city workers leave their families at home in the rural areas and migrate backwards and forwards.

While the majority of those migrating to Africa's cities do so voluntarily, Africa contains the world's greatest numbers of people who are forced to leave their homes. These are Africa's refugees, who now officially number over six million. It is estimated that there are a great many more 'unofficial refugees' or 'internally displaced' people.

Casablanca
3.2 (4.8)

Algiers
3.8 (6.4)

MOROCCO
27,377,000

ALGERIA
30,081,000

Alexandria
3.7 (5.4)

Cairo
9.9 (14.4)

EGYPT
65,978,000

SUDAN
28,292,000

NIGERIA
106,409,000

Ibadan
1.5 (3.0)

Lagos
10.9 (24.6)

ETHIOPIA
59,649,000

DEMOCRATIC REPUBLIC
OF CONGO
2,345,095

KENYA
29,008,000

Kinshasa
4.4 (9.4)

TANZANIA
32,102,000

Johannesburg
2.2 (3.4)

SOUTH
AFRICA
39,357,000

Cape Town
2.8 (4.4)

This map shows Africa's major cities with their populations (in millions) for 1996. The projected population for the year 2015 is in brackets. This map also shows the ten most populous states.

In 1994 Rwanda had nearly 2 million refugees living in neighbouring Zaire and Tanzania – these are Rwandan refugees at Kibumba camp, Goma in Zaire. There were also over 340,000 internally displaced people.

URBAN POPULATION STATISTICS

- In 1998, the total population of Africa was 748.9 million. By 2025, it is predicted to grow to 1.3 billion.

- Nigeria is the most populated country in Africa. In 1998, it was the tenth most-populated country in the world.

- Lagos is Africa's most populated city. In 1996, it was the world's twelfth most-populated city By 2015, it is estimated it will rise to third place.

- Between 1975–95, the city of Lagos more than doubled its population, growing by 212%. Lusaka, in Zambia, grew by 243% and Nairobi, in Kenya, grew by 167%.

- In 1996, Africa had two of the world's twenty largest cities – Lagos and Cairo (which is now one of the world's most densely settled megacities).

- In world terms, Africa has a low population density (number of people per km^2). In 1998, Africa had an average population density of 25 people per km^2. Compare this to Europe's average population density of 32 people, and Asia's 113 people per km^2.

- The African countries with the highest levels of population density are Rwanda (251), Burundi (232) and Nigeria (115).

- Africa now has thirty-seven cities with a population of over 1 million. In 1950, there were only two such cities.

- It is estimated that 79 per cent of the population of Addis Ababa live in slum areas; in Casablanca it is 70 per cent, Kinshasa 60 per cent and Cairo 60 per cent.

The number of Africans living in traditional family compounds, such as this one, decreases each year as more people move to the cities.

Is Africa Overpopulated?

In 1995, Africa had a population of over 680 million and this figure is expected to reach 1,500 million by the year 2025. The population is growing at an annual rate of 2.9 per cent, faster than in any other region of the world. The high growth rate is largely due to the fact that, while the number of births has continued to be high, the death rate has declined because of improved standards of living.

Many African countries face a huge challenge in finding resources to support the population growth, especially among young people and in the rapidly expanding cities. It is also a challenge to the world at large, because Africa is the world's poorest continent and will need considerable help. Some people argue that Africa is overpopulated and that if progress is to be achieved in future years, population numbers will have to come down. Others argue that Africa is actually underpopulated by world standards and that the problem is not the number of Africans, rather the poverty of so many.

VIEW 1:
AFRICA IS OVERPOPULATED

Today, Africa's population is growing faster than in any other part of the world. While there is some evidence that the rate of growth may slow down in the next decade or two, nonetheless Africa's population will reach at least 2.5 times what it is now within the next 30 years. There are very few African countries which have the resources to support this inevitable population explosion. The demands it will make on already underdeveloped health, education and sanitation services will be huge. This will inevitably mean that the quality of those services will decline even further.

It is feared that many African countries won't be able to adequately feed the expected increase in numbers. This problem is even more serious when we remember that it is the poor who have the largest families and the least ability to feed, clothe, shelter and educate them. People would not be so poor if they had fewer children.

While it's true that many parts of Africa are underpopulated, there is no doubt that an increasing number of areas – especially along the coast of West Africa, in parts of Eastern Africa, in countries like Rwanda and in many of Africa's rapidly growing towns and cities – are already overpopulated. Rapidly growing population numbers will place impossible demands on resources in those areas and will inevitably increase environmental damage.

Through education, we must encourage people to have smaller families. It is only through reducing the future numbers of Africans that we will be able to improve the quality of life on the continent.

VIEW 2:
AFRICA IS NOT OVERPOPULATED

Africa is well capable of feeding its own people and does so most of the time. It is only in extreme circumstances, sudden disasters or wars, that large numbers of people suffer from famine. There will be no problem in feeding Africa in the future if enough attention is given to producing food for local people.

As for those areas of Africa which are heavily populated today, much of this is due to the search for jobs and for a better life. If there were more jobs available and if services in rural areas were improved, fewer people would be tempted to move to the cities – thus reducing overcrowding. In the population debate, it's a mistake to concentrate on numbers only – it is equally important to look behind the numbers to other key issues.

Below *Services, such as this clinic, attract people to the cities and away from the rural areas which do not have such facilities.*

Below *Pie graphs showing world distribution of population in 1950, 1990 and 2025.*

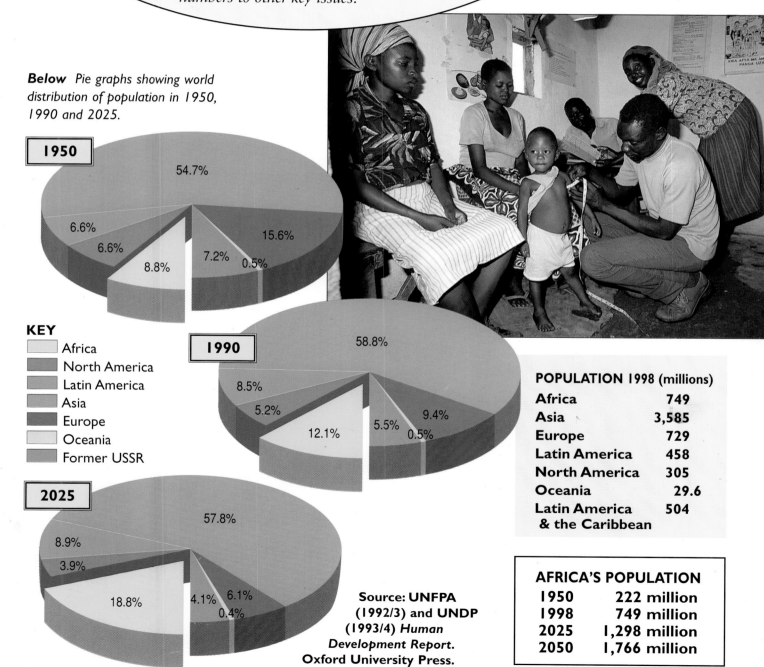

1950
- 54.7%
- 15.6%
- 0.5%
- 7.2%
- 8.8%
- 6.6%
- 6.6%

1990
- 58.8%
- 9.4%
- 0.5%
- 5.5%
- 12.1%
- 5.2%
- 8.5%

2025
- 57.8%
- 6.1%
- 0.4%
- 4.1%
- 18.8%
- 3.9%
- 8.9%

KEY
- Africa
- North America
- Latin America
- Asia
- Europe
- Oceania
- Former USSR

POPULATION 1998 (millions)	
Africa	749
Asia	3,585
Europe	729
Latin America	458
North America	305
Oceania	29.6
Latin America & the Caribbean	504

Source: **UNFPA** (1992/3) and **UNDP** (1993/4) *Human Development Report.* Oxford University Press.

AFRICA'S POPULATION	
1950	222 million
1998	749 million
2025	1,298 million
2050	1,766 million

HUMAN DEVELOPMENT

The images of Africa we see in the media and in the advertising of many voluntary agencies tend to be overwhelmingly negative. We often get the impression that little or no improvement has been made in the lives of ordinary Africans. However, while very real and life-threatening inequalities and problems continue to exist, real progress **has** been achieved in the areas of life expectancy, health, education, access to clean water, sanitation and nutrition.

The figures in the graphs (right) are average figures for all of Africa and hide crucial national differences. For instance, in 1992, the life expectancy of an average Mozambican was only 44 years (the worst in Africa), while that of the average Zimbabwean was 60 years (amongst the highest in Africa). The highest levels of adult literacy in 1990 were recorded in Algeria (93 per cent), with the lowest in Burkina Faso (18 per cent). There are also wide differences in the literacy rates for men and women.

Below An increasing number of children attend primary school.

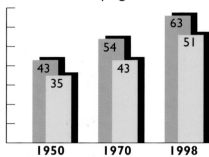

KEY TO GRAPHS
- Africa
- All developing countries

1950: 43 / 35
1970: 54 / 43
1998: 63 / 51

Life expectancy at birth (years)

Source: United Nations Development Project: Population World Trends, 1998

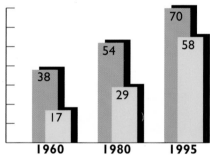

1960: 38 / 17
1980: 54 / 29
1995: 70 / 58

Adult literacy rate (Percentage of total population)

Source: UNICEF *State of the World's Children, 2000*

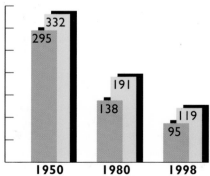

1950: 332 / 295
1980: 191 / 138
1998: 119 / 95

Under 5 years infant mortality rate (per 1000 births)

Source: UNICEF *State of the World's Children, 2000*

BALANCE SHEET OF HUMAN PROGRESS IN AFRICA

Achievement

In 1998, average life expectancy in Africa was 51 years, an increase of 10 years since 1960.

The under-5 infant mortality rate of 140 per 1000 births is over half what it was in 1960.

Two-thirds of all African countries have immunized 75 per cent of their children against major childhood diseases.

In urban areas, more than 80 per cent of children have access to safe drinking water. Clean water was provided to an additional 180 million Africans in the 1980s.

Many African countries experienced an overall increase in food production in the 1980s.

The numbers of those attending primary school in Africa rose dramatically in the 1970s and early 1980s.

In many African countries (eg. Niger, Angola, Malawi, Zambia, Ghana and Tunisia) the level of illiteracy amongst women has declined considerably.

With 10 per cent of world population in 1960–1965, the countries of sub-Saharan Africa had 12 per cent of the total world income.

Challenge

Africa's average life expectancy remains 20 years behind that of the industrialized world.

Children in Africa still die at a rate 10 times higher than that of the industrialised world.

Half of all Africans still have no access to basic healthcare.

Only 40 per cent of children have access to clean water in Africa's rural areas. Overall, 310 million still do not have access to clean water.

Overall food production in Africa declined in the 1980s and malnutrition affects about 30 per cent of African children.

Spending on education per person is roughly 20 times more in the industrialised countries and almost twice as high in Asia than in Africa.

Nearly 65 per cent of African women over the age of 15 are still illiterate, compared with 40 per cent of men.

Deteriorating economic conditions have meant that with 11 per cent of the world population in 1988–1989 these countries had only 7 per cent of the world income.

African states with high income levels	Gabon ($4,120) South Africa ($3,210) Botswana ($3,310)
medium income levels	Namibia ($2,110) Algeria ($1,500) Tunisia ($2,110)
low income levels	Ethiopia ($110) D.R of Congo ($110) Somalia ($110)

Source: UNICEF *State of the World's Children, 2000*

Right *Immunization against childhood diseases has dramatically reduced the infant mortality rate in many parts of Africa.*

CASE STUDIES IN AFRICAN HUMAN DEVELOPMENT

Africa is a continent of great diversity and contrast. Unfortunately, these differences often get lost in stories of war and famine. On the one hand, many African countries face serious human development problems, such as widespread hunger and malnutrition, war and conflict, lack of education and healthcare, and threats to the environment. But, on the other hand, much has been achieved, and this should not be forgotten.

How to measure human development is a matter of argument and debate. One traditional way is by Gross National Product (GNP) per capita. While this provides a glimpse of the theoretical average income per person, it tells us little about social or human development, or indeed about income distribution in any country. In recent years, other measurements of development have been introduced. These include the measurement of life expectancy, educational levels and infant mortality. This exercise has led the United Nations to develop what it calls the Human Development Index.

These three case studies illustrate some of the wide differences in development in Africa today and some of the key dimensions of both economic and social development.

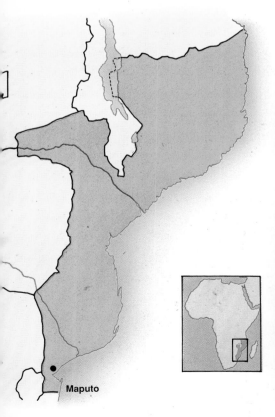

MOZAMBIQUE

Capital:	Maputo
Area:	799,380 km²
Population:	18,880,000
Literacy rate:	38%
Life expectancy:	44 yrs
Under 5 infant mortality rate (per 1000 births):	206
People living in absolute poverty:	59%

Mozambique is one of the world's very poorest countries. This is mostly due to a civil war which began in 1976 and only ended in October 1992. Between 1980 and 1991, food production per person declined by 23 per cent. Using almost all measures of development, Mozambique is one of the world's most vulnerable and least developed countries in human terms.

Below Mozambique is heavily dependent on food aid from Western countries.

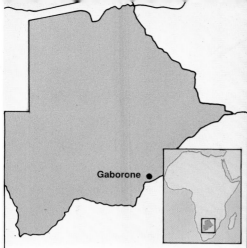

Right *Small-scale farms in Botswana are now growing a diversity of crops, such as tomatoes.*

BOTSWANA	
Capital:	Gaborone
Area:	582,000 km²
Population:	1,570,000
Literacy rate:	73%
Life expectancy:	47 yrs
Under 5 infant mortality rate (per 1000 births):	48
People living in absolute poverty:	43%

Measured on the Human Development Index, Botswana has been one of Africa's success stories in recent years. Its income per capita is one of the highest in Africa, while its literacy rate and infant mortality rate have improved steadily since 1960. In 1960, Botswana was at the bottom of the human development scale, but by 1992 it had climbed to the top of the medium levels of human development.

Despite experiencing frequent severe drought through the 1980s, Botswana succeeded in avoiding the worst effects of famine. This was achieved by combining outside food aid with the purchase of necessary foodstocks in South Africa and paying particular attention to the food needs of the poor and vulnerable.

ALGERIA	
Capital:	Algiers
Area:	2,381,741 km²
Population:	30,081,000
Literacy rate:	58%
Life expectancy:	69 yrs
Under 5 mortality rate (per 1000 births):	40
People living in absolute poverty:	23%

Algeria is one of North Africa's most developed countries, and was once a colony of France. Many of its achievements in recent years have been the result of its wealth in oil and gas reserves. Sharp increases in the price of oil in the early 1970s led to considerable growth in the economy. However, falling prices for oil and gas have led to serious losses of income and to many setbacks in human development.

Right *Much of Algeria's earnings abroad have come from the export of oil.*

FAMINE IN ETHIOPIA, 1984

Over 1 million people died in a famine in Ethiopia during 1984. The immediate cause of the famine was drought, though this was not the only reason. Drought has been a feature of many African countries during the twentieth century. In the past, people developed many different ways of dealing with it, but in 1984 the drought affected a people who were already vulnerable or at risk. A variety of causes came together to produce an immense famine.

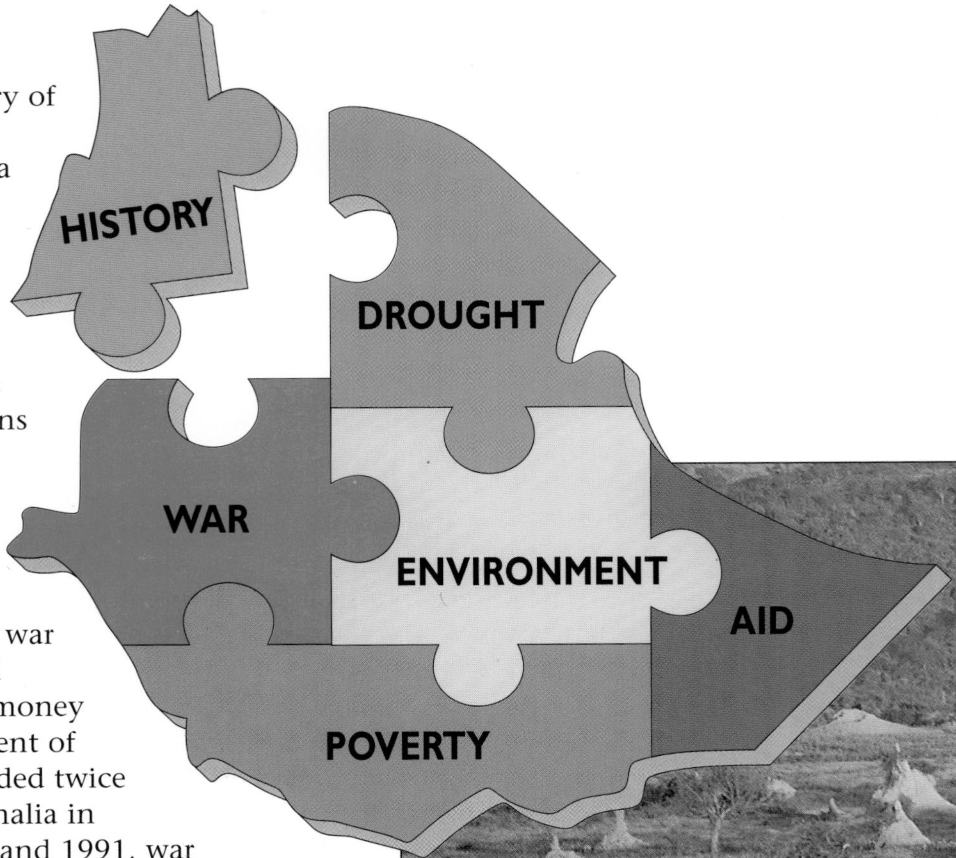

History

Ethiopia has a long history of famine and hunger. From 1930–1974, Ethiopia was ruled by Emperor Haile Selassie, who tried to modernize the country, but did little to reduce the poverty of its people. Many of his policies favoured the towns and the well-off and neglected agriculture and the poor.

War

In the twentieth century, war has continually disrupted agriculture and diverted money away from the development of Ethopia. It has been invaded twice (by Italy in 1935 and Somalia in 1977) and between 1961 and 1991, war continued in both Eritrea and Tigray, both of which fought to gain independence.

Poverty

Ethiopia is one of the world's poorest countries. Average yearly income in 1984 was only $110 per capita. The food supplies of the majority of Ethiopians are very limited and they depend heavily on each harvest. Few have reserves of food or cash to support themselves in times of drought or war, and many are vulnerable to food insecurity and eventually famine.

HISTORY

DROUGHT

WAR

ENVIRONMENT

AID

POVERTY

Drought

Severe drought occurred in Ethiopia in 1972 to 1974, in 1975, 1979 and again in 1980. Between 1980 and 1982, the rains in some places were less than one third the normal amount. In 1983 there was an almost total failure of the rains that are so important for the production of local food crops. Rains were again very poor in 1984.

Above *This is one of the relief centres set up for famine victims.*

Below *This refugee camp is in Moyale, Ethiopia.*

Environment

Deforestation and soil erosion were also contributing factors to the famine. In 1884, 44 per cent of Ethiopia was wooded, but by 1984 this figure was down to 4 per cent. The United Nations estimated that Ethiopia was losing 1.6 billion tonnes of soil each year in the early 1980s. Population growth also contributed to environmental damage as more and more people sought to make a living from the land.

Aid

In 1981, 1982 and 1983, the Ethiopian government warned of the dangers of famine and the need for food aid from international sources. Despite this appeal, aid was very slow in arriving and never came in large enough quantities to prevent widespread hunger. Aid to build up roads and airstrips was also slow in arriving, and this hindered food aid distribution.

VULNERABILITY

Poor people who are at risk of hunger and poor countries that are at risk of famine are often said to be vulnerable, that is, their ability to resist or overcome shortages, droughts, floods or disease is very limited or non-existent. Understanding vulnerability is often the key to understanding why famines occur.

ENVIRONMENT

Africa is suffering from a serious environmental crisis that badly affects the lives of many people. Overall, about 3.7 million hectares of useful land are lost each year. The United Nations now estimates that nearly a quarter of the whole continent is in danger of becoming useless as a result of soil erosion and deforestation.

DEFORESTATION

At the beginning of the 1990s, the world was using about two-and-a-half times as much wood as it did in 1950. By the early 1970s, up to one-third of the world's tropical rain forests had been lost and cutting was progressing at the rate of $100,000 \, km^2$ per annum. By the early 1990s, this had almost doubled, to about $170,000 \, km^2$ a year.

About half of the world's timber production annually is used for producing fuelwood and charcoal in developing countries. Increasing populations have led to increased demand and as other forms of energy are beyond the means of most people in these countries, fuelwood consumption is expected to continue to rise. The production and use of charcoal, which is made from wood, causes the release of carbon dioxide into the atmosphere.

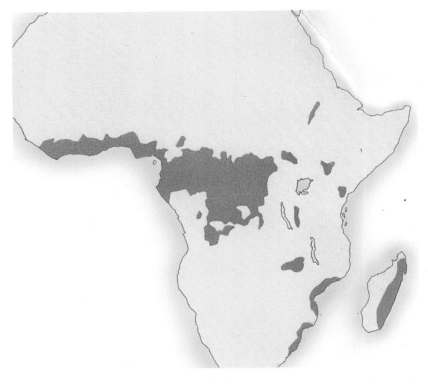

Above This map shows areas threatened by deforestation. Logging has caused serious damage to irreplaceable ecosystems throughout the world. In West Africa, 4 per cent of forest land is being lost each year. Tree loss contributes greatly to soil erosion, which in turn has major implications for agriculture.

Left Cattle are herded towards their pasture in East Africa; Mount Kenya looms in the background. Overgrazing by cattle herds has stripped the land of its grass in parts of Africa.

SOIL EROSION

Each year, the world's deserts grow by 6 million hectares. A further 1.0 to 1.5 million hectares are lost through salinity and waterlogging. Erosion, overploughing, overgrazing, poor irrigation and other poor farming practices are making an area larger than that of England unproductive each year. About 26 billion tonnes of topsoil is lost annually. Throughout Africa, more soil is being lost than is being created. In some areas, soil loss is so bad that it creates rock-hard layers that cannot be worked with hand tools or be penetrated by plant roots. Crop yields are falling and wood for fuel is declining.

Projects are underway to reverse this trend. Irrigation schemes, re-afforestation and terracing (to prevent soil loss) are all part of modern agriculture. Training courses stress the importance of respect for nature and for the land. Many Africans are deeply concerned about environmental issues, but point out that these are directly related to the issue of poverty, and that this will have to be tackled as part of the overall approach to protecting the environment.

Pressure on habitats is driving 100 species of plants and animals to extinction each day. Scientists are concerned that, each day, the results of millions of years of evolution are being destroyed without anyone having investigated them properly. By the early 1990s only 600,000 African elephants remained, their numbers decimated by ivory poachers. This herd of elephants is in Addo Elephant Park in South Africa.

HOW ENVIRONMENTAL CONDITIONS AFFECT DEVELOPMENT

lack of rainfall	spells of drought (poor crop yields), years of drought (hunger), prolonged and regular drought, eg. in the Sahel
rainfall in storms	leaching of the nutrients in the soil, erosion, high water loss
low clay content in many soils	high levels of erosion, poor ability to retain water and nutrients, leading to low fertility
variable weather patterns	extra agricultural work and high levels of weed growth, crop losses through disease and pests
low surface water availability and few sources of shallow groundwater	high labour input in carrying water and high cost of irrigation

AFRICA IN THE WORLD

In the past, Africa played a major role in world trade. However, in recent years Africa's share of trade has declined to below 3 per cent of world total. The price of the goods that Africa exports (coffee, cotton, copper and cocoa) have declined, while those of the goods it imports (oil, consumer goods and machinery) have all increased. African countries need the income earned by exports to pay for investment in agriculture, industry and health. Many African leaders argue for a change in trade policy. This will mean higher prices for some goods that Europeans have been able to buy cheaply in the past.

Africans represent little more than 11 per cent of the world's total population, but they have made a tremendous contribution to our universal heritage. In art and literature, in sport and trade, today's Africans have much to offer. African art has had a very considerable influence on American and European artists, many of whom have drawn inspiration from the vibrant traditional arts of Africa. African masks, design, sculpture and jewellery are particularly distinctive. Much world music draws its inspiration from African music and rhythms.

Douglas Wakihuru is one of many Kenyan athletes who have excelled in world sport.

WANGARI MAATHAI

In 1989, Professor Wangari Maathai was presented with the international 'Woman of the World' award. This was in recognition of her setting up the Green Belt Movement in Kenya. Professor Wangari Maathai realised that a large number of trees in Kenya had already been destroyed and that more cash crops would only increase the problem. In her work over 14 years, she had persuaded communities throughout Kenya to plant more than 10 million trees and, in response to her success, another thirty-five African countries have adopted the scheme. Women in Kenya have also pioneered the collection of seeds from local trees and have developed nurseries based upon them. Such actions, as well as the many others promoted by the Green Belt Movement, have helped to tackle key environmental issues.

CHINUA ACHEBE (born 1930)

The Nigerian writer, Chinua Achebe, first became famous for his book *Things Fall Apart*, published in 1958. In the book, a tribal leader returns to his tribe after many years, only to find that the old ways of life are disappearing fast, to be replaced by modern ideas and ways of living that have their origins in other cultures. In other novels and short stories written since that time, Achebe has continued to present an image of the traditional life of his own people and to examine how their culture is threatened.

LÉOPOLD SÉDAR SENGHOR (born 1906)

Léopold Sédar Senghor was born in an area that was then called French West Africa (now Senegal). As the name tells us, this part of Africa was a French colony and Senghor received part of his education in Paris. He fought in the French Army during the Second World War, but was captured and spent some years in a German prisoner-of-war camp. Senghor became widely known following the publication of his first volume of poetry *Chants d'ombre* (*Shadow Songs*) in 1945. Later, he became a member of the French National Assembly and began to work for Senegalese independence.

When Senegal became independent in 1960, Senghor became his country's first president, an office which he held until he retired in 1980. In 1984, he became the first black person to be honoured with membership of the French Academy.

WOLE SOYINKA (born 1934)

The Nigerian Wole Soyinka, writes poetry, novels and plays. Although he writes mostly in English, Soyinka uses the myths and legends of the Yoruba people in his work.

Below *Wole Soyinka was the first African to be awarded the Nobel prize for literature.*

BOUTROS BOUTROS-GHALI (born 1922)

Between 1992–96, Boutros Boutros-Ghali was Secretary-General of the United Nations, one of the most important jobs in the world. Boutros-Ghali studied in Africa, Europe and America before he became active in politics in his native Egypt. He played an important role in resolving conflict between Egypt and Israel and also intervened to help bring peace in other African conflicts. In 1997, another African, Ghana-born Kofi Annan took over his position as Secretary-General.

Left *Boutros-Ghali was the first African and the first Arab to be given the post of Secretary-General of the UN.*

TIMELINE

BC

4000 Early settlements along the banks of the Nile.

3500 Kingdom of the Pharaohs established on the Nile.

2500 Metal-using cultures appear along coast of North Africa.

1000 Early cultivation present in both East and West Africa. Bantu-speaking Africans spread outwards from North Africa.

671 Assyrian conquest of Egypt.

520 Darius I completes canal connecting the Nile with the Red Sea.

334 Alexander the Great conquers Egypt.

30 Death of Antony and Cleopatra. Egypt becomes a Roman province.

AD

44 Morocco annexed by Rome.
429 Vandal kingdom in North Africa.

641 Arabs conquer Egypt and begin conquest of North Africa.

700–800 Arabs conquer North Africa and convert the local people to Islam. Arab traders establish trading towns on the east coast.

969 Fatimids conquer Egypt and found Cairo.

1135 Almohads dominant in northwest Africa and Muslim Spain.

1171 Saladin defeats Fatimids and conquers Egypt.

1228 Hafsid dynasty established at Tunis.

1400s European explorers seeking a sea route to Asia discover much of the African coast and trade with African tribes, bringing gold and ivory to Europe.

1498 Portuguese explorer, Vasco da Gama, rounds the Cape of Good Hope and sails on to India. Portuguese introduce Christianity to large parts of Africa.

1500s Other European powers become involved in Africa and begin to take over part of the Portuguese trade.

1546 Destruction of the Mali empire by Songhay.

1571 Portuguese create colony in Angola.

1578 Moroccans destroy Portuguese power in northwest Africa.

1591 Moroccans destroy Songhay kingdom.

1652 Foundation of Cape Colony by Dutch.

1659 French found trading station on Senegal coast.

1662 Battle of Ambuila: destruction of Kongo kingdom by Portuguese.

1700 Rise of Asante power (Gold coast).

1730 Revival of ancient empire of Borno (central Sudan).

1798 Napolean attacks Egypt.

1800–1914 Africa divided between the French, Belgians, Portuguese, British, Germans and Italians.

1807 Slave trade abolished within the British Empire.

1811 Mohammed Ali takes control in Egypt.

1818 Shaka forms Zulu kingdom in southeast Africa.

1822 Liberia founded as colony for freed slaves.

1830 French begin conquest of Algeria.

1835 'Great Trek' of Boer colonists from Cape, leading to foundation of Republic of Natal(1839), Orange Free State (1848) Transvaal (1849).

1840s Livingstone's explorations begin.

1860 French expansion in West Africa from Senegal.

1869 Suez Canal opens.

1875 Disraeli buys Suez Canal Company shares to ensure British control of sea route to India.

1881 French occupy Tunisia.

1882 Revolt in Egypt leading to British occupation.

1884 Germany acquires southwest Africa.

1885 King of Belgium acquires Congo.

1886 Germany and Britain partition East Africa. Gold is discovered in Transvaal, and Johannesburg is founded.

1889 British South Africa Company formed by Cecil Rhodes, begins colonization of Rhodesia (1890).

1896 Italians defeated by Ethiopians.

1898 Fashoda crisis between Britain and France.

1899 Boer War begins.

1900–1960 African nationalism and desire for independence grows with opposition to colonial rule.

1908 Belgian state takes over Congo from King Leopold of Belgium.

1910 Foundation of Union of South Africa.

1912 Italy conquers Libya.

1914–15 French and British conquer German colonies except German East Africa.

1919 Nationalist revolt in Egypt against the British.

1930-1975 Forty-one African states become independent.

1935 Italy invades Ethiopia.

1936 Anglo-Egyptian alliance.

1940 Italians expelled from Somalia, Eritrea and Ethiopia.

1942 Germans advance into Egypt. Battle of El-Alamein: German retreat and defeat. Anglo-American landings in Morocco and Algeria.

1949 Apartheid introduced in South Africa.

1952 Beginning of Mau Mau rebellion in Kenya. Military revolt in Egypt.

1956 Beginning of decolonization in sub-Saharan Africa: Gold Coast becomes independent.

1960 'Africa's year'. Many states become independent.

1961 South Africa becomes an independent republic.

1962 Algeria becomes independent.

1965 Rhodesia declares independence.

1967 Civil war in Nigeria.

1975 Portugal grants independence to Mozambique and Angola.

1980 Black majority rule in Zimbabwe (Rhodesia).

1984 Famine in Sahel and Ethiopia.

1985 Civil unrest in South Africa.

1986 US bomb Libya for terrorist activities.

1990 Namibia becomes independent. The South African government recognizes the ANC, frees Nelson Mandela and, in 1991, starts to dismantle apartheid.

1992 US forces intervene to end Somalia's famine and civil war.

1994 President Mandela becomes president of South Africa in the country's first democratic elections.

1198 Civil war breaks out in the Democratic Republic of Congo.

1999 Nigeria successfully elects its first civilian government after fifteen years of military rule.

2000 President Nelson Mandela steps down as president of South Africa.

GLOSSARY

Administration How a country or organization is run or managed.

ANC African National Congress – a political party which fought in South Africa for the rights of black Africans and an end to apartheid.

Apartheid A policy of segregating white and black South Africans which was dismantled in 1991.

Colonialism A policy and practice of stronger countries taking over control of weaker countries.

Culture Aspects of a country or society that make it distinctive – its way of life, art, music and religion.

Democratic System of government or decision-making through a voting system open to all.

Discrimination To treat different groups (eg. ethnic or religious groups) differently, usually to their disadvantage.

Domestic needs What a country needs in terms of goods and materials to satisfy the requirements of its own people.

Drought An extended period of very low rainfall. Often resulting, in Africa, in poor crop growth and famine.

Economy System of production of goods and services; distribution of income, exchange with other countries and consumption.

Ethnic origin Refers to the original place of origin of a person or their ancestors.

Export The sale of goods or services from one country to another.

Famine A severe shortage of food resulting from crop failure or overpopulation.

Fertilizer Chemicals or manure added to the soil to improve the growth of crops.

GNP Gross National Product – the total value of all goods and services produced each year by a country. Often referred to as 'GNP per capita' which means the total value of annual sales of goods and services divided by the population of the country. The higher the GNP per capita, the wealthier the country.

Immunize To help stop people catching diseases by injecting them with antibodies or very mild forms of the disease.

Integration The merging of peoples, cultures or economies to become more unified.

Intensive farming Farming involving high concentrations of animals or wide-spread use of agricultural chemicals.

Investment Money spent by governments, industry or individuals to support development of a product or service; a 'return' on the investment is usually expected.

Media Newspaper, radio, television and any other means of spreading news and information to large numbers of people.

Menial Something – usually work – which needs little skill.

Migration Moving from one place to another to find better conditions for living or feeding.

Nutrition Related to the intake of food and nutrients required to survive.

Plantation An estate or large area where crops are grown for sale.

Refugee A person who has run away from some danger or problem such as famine or war.

Republic A country that has no king or queen and therefore often has a president and a prime minister.

Resources Usually refers to the naturally-occurring materials available to a country, eg. coal, iron ore, forest, fish.

Safari park An enclosed park where lions and other non-native wild animals can be allowed to roam free and where people can look at them from the safety of their cars.

Salinity The level of salt in something – often in water.

Standard of living The level of wealth and services available to citizens for living, in terms of education, healthcare, goods, etc.

Subsidy Payment, usually by government, to support a particular activity, eg. farming.

Subsistence farming A type of farming where most of the produce is used for the consumption of the farmer's family.

Tribe A group of people with a common ethnic origin.

Urbanized Where a large proportion of the population is concentrated in towns and cities.

Weathering Process by which rocks and landscapes are changed by wind, rain, etc.

FURTHER INFORMATION

Non-fiction for children

Crisis in Central Africa (New Perspectives series) (Hodder Wayland, 1999)

East Africa (World Fact Files series) (Hodder Wayland, 1997)

Egypt (Country Fact Files series*)* (Hodder Wayland, 1996)

A Flavour of Kenya by Wambui Kairi (Hodder Wayland, 1999)

Kenya (Country Insights series) by Wambui Kairi (Wayland, 1997)

Life Stories: Nelson Mandela (Hodder Wayland, 1993)

Philips Geographical Digest 2000 (Heinemann Educational, 2000)

Southern Africa (World Fact Files series*)* (Hodder Wayland, 1997)

Stories from Africa (Hodder Wayland, 2000)

Traditions from Africa (Cultural Journeys series) (Hodder Wayland, 1998)

Wayland Atlas of Threatened Cultures (Hodder Wayland, 2000)

West Africa (World Fact Files series*)*(Hodder Wayland, 1997)

Non-fiction reference material

Philips Geographical Digest 2000 (Heinemann Educational, 2000)

Addresses and websites

ActionAid, Hamlyn House, Archway, London N19 5PG. Tel: 0207 282 4101 Website: www.actionaid.org

Africa.com   Website: www.africa.com

Oxfam: 274 Banbury Road, Oxford OX2 7DZ. Tel: 01865 56777   Website: www.oxfam.org.uk

Development Education Association, 3rd Floor, Cowper Street, London EC2A 4AP

MBendi: Information for Africa   Website: http://mbendi.co

United Nations Development Programme   Website: www.undp.org

Unicef: 55-6 Lincoln's Inn Fields, London WC2A 3NB. Tel: 0207 405 5592 Website: www.unicef.org

Novels

There are a great many fine African novelists, whose books give a good idea of what different aspects of African life are like. Most of their work is more suitable for older readers, but some of these books would be very interesting for younger children. Chinua Achebe (*Things Fall Apart*, *Petals of Blood*) is a good place to start, since his books are often quite short and deal with subjects everyone can understand, such as what happens when your country is invaded by people from elsewhere. Achebe's novels usually have a list of other Afrcian novelists and their books on the final pages.

Older readers might be interested to read Barry Unsworth's *Sacred Hunger*, which is about the effects of the slave trade on all those involved in it, and no list of books to read of Africa could be complete without mentioning *Heart of Darkness* by Joseph Conrad, which deals with the effect Africa had on its early European colonizers.

INDEX

The figures in **bold** refer to photographs